'Twas the night before New Year's
and all held their breath
for the year that held promise
to outbest the best.

All vision would be perfect,
all things would be clear,
and the business success we had chased
would come near.

Published by Sir Brody Books, sirbrody.com
Illustrated by Hendra Hitam
Copyright 2020, D.K. Brantley
ISBN: 978-1-951551-15-5

Then a couple months passed and a strange thing occurred:

A virus arrived like a flaming bag of dog turds.

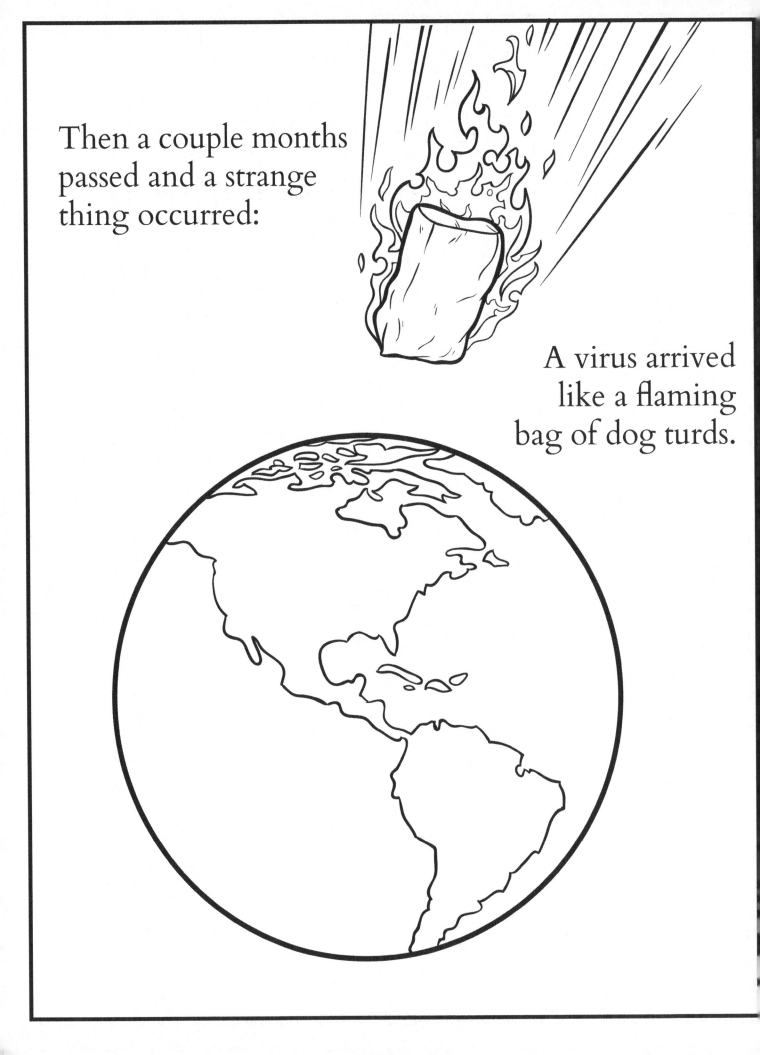

Well, we stomped on the bag,
tried putting it out,
but the virus
did not seem phased.

Even less did it care when we turned our backs, pretending it would just go away.

But not all were content
to ignore the new bug
or act like it didn't exist.

Some folks spoke up,
confident they could see
clear facts that others had missed.

"It's China!" they screamed.
"They made this in a lab!"
And the idea seemed fairly legit.

Politicians agreed
it was likely they had,
but what could they do about it?

Not much, it seemed,
could slow new COVID down,
and in time, all our smiles
were transformed into frowns.

Desperate, we begged COVID,
"Leave our land!"

It refused.

So we hoarded toilet paper,
masked up, washed our hands.

(Or at least some of us did.)

But the story of 2020
can't be reduced to a virus.

Other murder hornet–esque elements
were equally undesirous*.

*According to m-w.com, undesirous *is not the appropriate word here, as it means "lacking desire" or "feeling no desire." However, I trust the good-looking, smart, and humble users of this coloring book understand the sentiment I hoped to achieve with the word* undesirous *and will forgive this misstep. Besides, this ain't exactly Shakespeare. If it were, I would make up a word to fit my needs. But that's a lesson for another day. Anyway, enjoy the rest of the book!*

Racial tensions, riots, violence,
opportunistic looters,
people staying at home who had
long been commuters.

They mourned their jobs
that went up in smoke,
half the nation overnight became
suddenly broke.

Thankfully in the midst of this yearlong cesspit was one tiny, beautiful bit of respite:

THE UNITED STATES PRESIDENTIAL ELECTION

From the start this election
was surely unique,
two elderly frontrunners
both poised to critique.

Outdated names were called,
ancient insults spoken,
and while COVID struck one,
no septuagenarian bones were broken.

Election day came, and it came with a

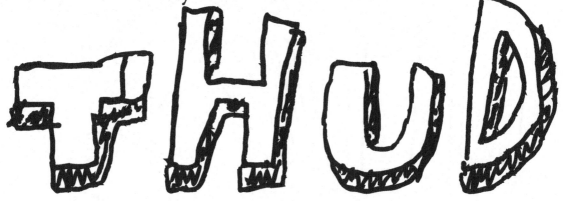

reminding all citizens of the bad

between commies and racists, elite and enlightened.

Who's who?
We're not sure.
The similarities are frightening.

Adding flame and fuel to the
poo-filled bag on fire,
some states didn't know
how to count any higher
than twenty.

So a waiting game ensued.

Somehow, someway, the counting came to an end.

A new president was chosen and prepared to ascend.

Relief in the air, the decision made,
the losing party resigned
to spend four years afraid.

But the momentum was slowed
and then came to a halt
as the second-place candidate
deemed the election a fraud.

Attorneys worked lickety split on the case,
hungry to end this exhausting

race.

Their hard work paid off
and after many long days,
the new president was
once and for all, finally named.

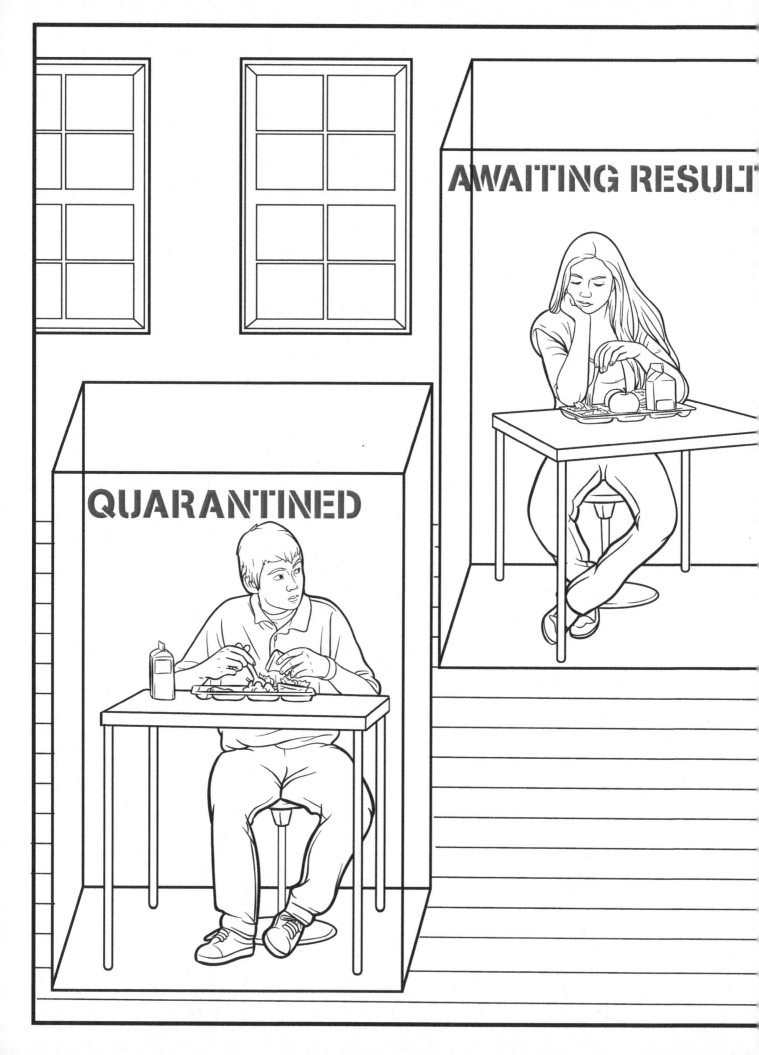

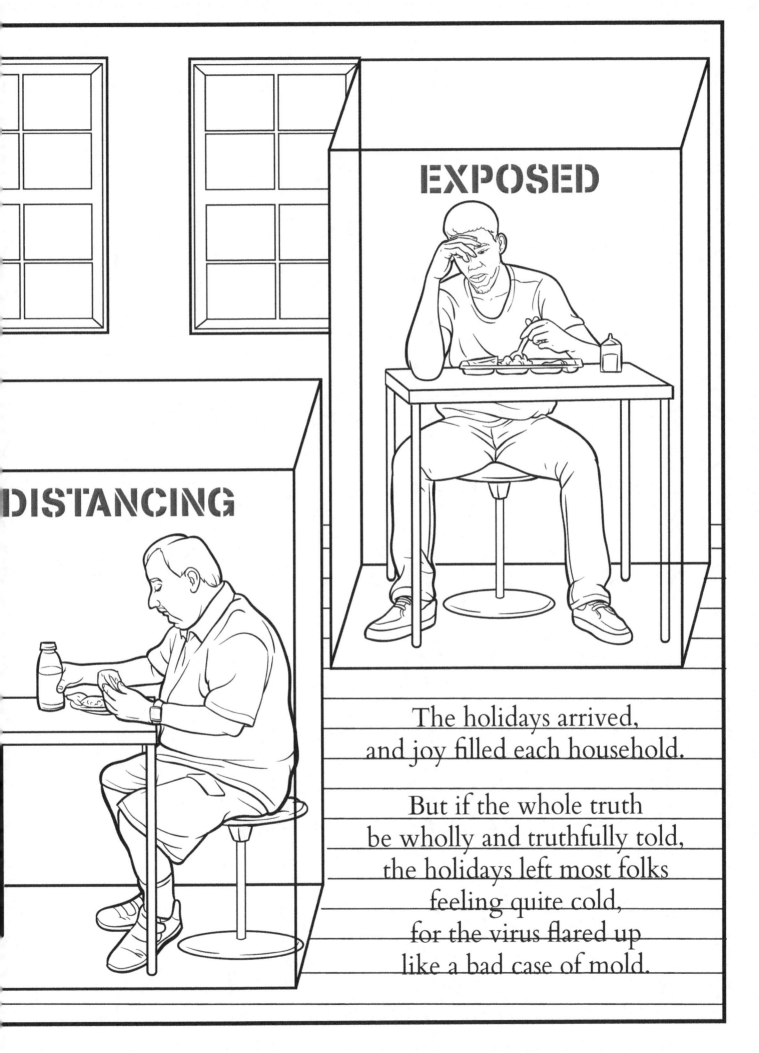

EXPOSED

DISTANCING

The holidays arrived,
and joy filled each household.

But if the whole truth
be wholly and truthfully told,
the holidays left most folks
feeling quite cold,
for the virus flared up
like a bad case of mold.

As 2020 reached its dramatic, slow close,
all hoped the year's thorns
would produce next year's rose.

Let's hope they're right.

Enjoy this trip down memory lane?

Leave an online review, so others can relive the pain
of the fears and the tension that were aplenty
in the historically agonizing year, 2020.

*P.S. Wish you could color this again and again and again? Go to sirbrody.com/2020 to download a FREE PDF
of the entire book. Then print the pages you love most and color them again and again until you get it just right.*

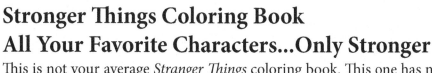

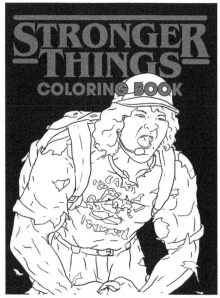

Stronger Things Coloring Book
All Your Favorite Characters...Only Stronger

This is not your average *Stranger Things* coloring book. This one has more. A LOT more...MUSCLE!

That's right—this book doesn't have ANY wimpy pictures to color. Every one of them features a musclebound character that's sure to get you PUMPED.

A great gift for fans of *Stranger Things*, this coloring book will be loved by kids and adults alike, but should be avoided by anyone who is intimidated by muscle PILED on top of muscle.

Featuring more than 50 original, hilariously powerful illustrations of your favorite *Stranger Things* characters, this coloring book gives what you didn't know you needed: beefed-up characters doing AWESOME stuff.

Cats Doing Things Coloring Book:
50 pictures of cute cats that are fun & easy for all ages to color

Cat kids, cat ladies, and cat dudes alike love this one-of-a-kind coloring book made just for them.

If you've been looking for a coloring book that shows the secret lives of your favorite furry creatures, look no further! These 50 pictures show cats doing what they typically only do in secret—skateboarding, gardening, karate chopping, scuba diving, and more!

With 50 pictures of cats doing things, this book is perfect for kids and adults, ages 2 through 102, though younger and older enjoy it as well.

Dig dinosaurs? Don't miss *Dinosaurs Doing Things Coloring Book*!

The Only Magic Book You'll Never Need
By D.K. Brantley

It's funny, hilarious, clever, and magical. But it's far from useful.

Written by a magical dimwit, *The Only Magic Book You'll Never Need* has been lovingly called "100 pages of fantastic nonsense."

In it, you'll learn how to cauterize a severed torso, turn friends into enemies using super glue and headphones, and more.

Becoming an illusionist has never been so impossible, dangerous, and funny.

Sample from Stronger Things Coloring Book

Made in the USA
Monee, IL
21 December 2020